A RAINBOW BABY STORY
THE RAINBOW AFTER THE STORM

WRITTEN BY
CRYSTAL FALK AND KIM ROMAN

What is a Rainbow Baby?

A rainbow baby is a baby who is born after a parent has experienced a miscarriage, stillbirth or infant loss.

The thought is, the loss is like a storm and the baby who follows is like the rainbow. After a storm, a rainbow filled with hope may appear. Although there are still dark clouds above, there is hope and joy that follows the storm.

NOTE: Most mental health care experts believe that death should be explained briefly but honestly to young children. The words chosen fall in line with that thinking.

Add your special angel(s) here:

_____

Add your special rainbow(s) here:

_____

For Katelyn , Luther and Reece

A Special Thank You to Gina Ashline
for giving of her professional editing services.

Angel Babies

Aubriella Holcomb

Parker Thomas Kauer

Riley and Angel Leska

Christopher James

Baby Somorin

Baby Harkness

Liam Walsh

Baby Skylar

Anthony Michael

Megan Owens

Baby Yoder

Vincenzo James

Baby Smithers

Baby Burkett

Baby Holcomb

Jacob

Weston

Grayson

Peanut

Caden

Baby Hibbs

Baby Case

Baby Wolfe

Baby Angel

Baby Owens

Baby Owens

Aiden Slaugh

Baby Haevy

"All children are miracles, even the ones that couldn't stay very long."

- Author unknown

Rainbow Babies

Kiarra Faith Wheeler

Falyn Shyne McKeachie

Emily Owens

Justice Orio

Azelyn

Baby H.

Morgan Mallory

Chayton Reed

Nigel S

Baby Nova

Jordan Om

Allyson Rayne

Hunter Lockhart

Michael Jay

Brantley and Paisley Mae

Baby Davis

Asiya Estrada-Young

Baby Horizyn

Camren and Timothy Smithers

Massimo Alboretto

Nic

Mathew Magrath

Karson

Baby Kauer

Mercedes james

Kate

Matthews Family

"There is a Rainbow of Hope After Every Storm"

- Author unknown

Angel Babies

Sofia Carol Martin

Carol Theeny-Smith

Savanna Faith Hamilton

Paityn Marie B.

Paisley Anne B.

Kaiden Banks

Chloe

Isabella Rose

Jax Carter

Jurnee Estrada

Junior

Mathieu Babies

Michael

Taylor Lee and Tyler Mae Banks

Roman Babies

Molly Ann Banks

Dream Marie

Sierra Isabella

Jellybean

Pistachio M

Brandon

Toby lee Magrath

Silas Elijah B.

Baby Karlsen

Baby Gunder

"All children are miracles, even the ones that couldn't stay very long."

- Author unknown

Rainbow Babies

Mariah Hope Bickford and Ciara Marie Leatzau

Alija Christopher Quirindongo

Gwyneth M

Journey Dream

Olivia Rose

Tina

Kyle

Baby Hamilton

Sinatra Banks

Hayden James Edwards

Brentlee Jaxon

Janette Banks

Lincoln Charlie

Dexter J Forslund

Nathan Banks

Matthew & Jeremy R.

Greyson Banks

Jasmine Nevaeh and Eli James

Courtney

Savannah Rose Papineau

Baby Baty

Chloe Leilani Marjorie Harman

Tobias M.

Alyssa Anne B.

Tabitha M.

Tracy

Steven Dell

"There is a Rainbow of Hope After Every Storm"

- Author unknown

Angel Babies

Scarlett Rayne, Nevaeh,
Peanut, & Kayden Xavier

Alexandria Grace
and Melanie Dawn

Lily Marie-Jean Copp

Baby Cathey

Baby Edwards

Dragonfly

Baby Watts

Hope Larsen

Sebastian Isaiah

Nur Farook

Baby Engle-Grisby

L.B.

Violet Lynea Romero

Jonah Isaiah

Claire Christine

Dason Griffin

Diego Cedrick Brede

Mia Arabella Romero-Hunter

Austin James Taylor

Ava Rose Bonadio

Athena Rose Larsen

Daniel Luis Anzures

Elena Rosalie Larsen

Elijah Alexand Larsen

Stephen Alexan Larsen

"All children are miracles, even the
ones that couldn't stay very long."

- Author unknown

Rainbow Babies

Sarah and Joe Smithenson

Madilyn Beth Coverdale

Allison

Steve

Majid John Shah Farook

Baby Bryan

Arya Marie Glass

Xayden Xavier

Lacee Ameera Bonadio

Thomas O'Neil

Zack Keelan Norman

Rayhan Walsh Mungur

Jack Lincoln

Nathaniel Josiah Wills

Jackson Dale Romero

Falyn Shyne McKeachie

Jackson

Braydin Aaron Schreiner

Baby Elijah Eugene Cathey

Dio Lee Jr.

Kamden Lee-Calvin Germer

Hayden James Edwards

Xavier Jaydin Watts

Emmalee Grace Bunke

Tony

Payton Antoinette Page

"There is a Rainbow of Hope After Every Storm"
- Author unknown

Angel Babies

Arabella Marie Glass

Ayden Lauren Glass

Baby D and Isabelle Corinne

Matthew Brennan Coverdale

Rose Oleary

Alexis Nicole Crane

Hope Oleary

April Oleary

Harvie-lee Wheeler

Stephiney Lee Ann

Baby Josh

Harper & Elle Bunke

Alani Rose Harman

Mason Adrian Diaz

Owen Ramsey Bunke

Antoine Mason Laney Page

Audrianna Grace Raybourn

Bronte Elizebeth Lee

Jay Michael McClung

Tom N.

Timothy Wayne Davidson

Skylar Harris Slaymaker

Finley Lynn Goodwillie

Dylann Nathaniel Will

Callie-Mae Rose Ramsey

Keelan Davi Gordon Gillingha

"All children are miracles, even the
ones that couldn't stay very long."

- Author unknown

Rainbow Babies

Edward L. Johnson

Megan and Charles Toms

Eva Drumm

Katie Baby Reed

Jack and Carly

Carrie S

Chris

Chadwick N

Madison Jumper

Christina

Gail Smith

John T Smith

Susan

Thomas Saunders

Lee Davis

Herbert Williams

Clark Ebbe

Veronica and Chrissy

Anton Holder

Alex

Ben Thompson

Paula

Robert D.

James P

Michael

Emily Wingler

"There is a Rainbow of Hope
After Every Storm"
- Author unknown

Once upon a time a family of birds lived in a nest high up in a tree. In the nest lived Momma Bird, Daddy Bird and Baby Bird. Their nest was cozy and warm, lined with soft feathers.

Baby Bird loved their nest and all the beautiful bright green trees around it.

One day while Momma Bird was out getting lunch, the wind started blowing, the clouds grew dark and it began to rain.

A storm had come.

Before Momma Bird got back, the storm grew strong and thunder shook their nest. Baby Bird was very scared. He had never seen a big storm.

Momma Bird returned to their nest and protected him from the storm.
He snuggled up next to her underneath her wing.

She began to tell Baby Bird that although storms can be scary and can cause a lot of sadness, storms can also bring something beautiful... sometimes they bring rainbows.

While Momma Bird was explaining to Baby Bird that storms may pass, the rain stopped and the sun peeked through the clouds.

As the sun shined through the clouds, a beautiful rainbow appeared.

"Baby Bird, although rainbows are colorful and bring joy and hope, we will never forget the storm that came before the rainbow."

"Before Mommy and Daddy had you in our nest, we had another egg. We were so happy to be having a little baby bird. Day after day we waited for our Little Baby Bird to hatch from her egg."

"One day she stopped growing. She did not grow big and strong like you did and, sadly, she died. When birds die, they stop breathing. They no longer chirp or flap their wings. And this is what happened to Little Baby Bird."

"All things that have life eventually die, but it's especially sad if it happens before the egg even hatches or if they are very young.

Just like you during the storm, we were scared and very sad."

"Many years after Little Baby Bird died, we found out we were going to have you. The day you hatched from your egg was the day we felt joy and happiness again. You are our Rainbow Baby Bird. You brought us joy and hope after the terrible storm."

"We will never forget our first egg and we will love her forever."

"Sometimes scary winds will blow and dark clouds will be above us.
But we must always hope that it will be followed by a beautiful rainbow."

"There isn't always a rainbow after a storm, but when there is, we appreciate it even more. And that is the beauty of the rainbow after a storm."

About the Authors

Crystal Falk has been writing children's books on sensitive subjects since she became a surrogate mother in 2013. Her educational background in art, graphic design and creative writing as well as her experience with sensitive topics gives her a unique perspective which she incorporates into her writing. When Crystal is not writing children's books, she is caring for her three preschoolers and spending time with her husband.

Kim Roman is an Air Force veteran, former home school mom and Oma to Katelyn, Luther and Reece. She and her husband Tim have several Angel Babies and two Rainbow Babies who are now adults. She is the owner of Square Foot Gardening 4 U and teaches small-space organic vegetable gardening. She is a Square Foot Gardening Certified Instructor and enjoys working with non-profit organizations, homeless shelters and schools to help improve the health of others. Kim is a member of the Garden Writers Assoc.

Made in the USA
San Bernardino, CA
20 July 2017